Paul Collison is a poet from Wales. He has been writing for many years and this is his first publication. He enjoys music and movies in his spare time.

He lives in the valleys of South Wales with his wife Julie and pet cats, and enjoys walking in the mountains and visiting places of interest for inspiration.

My Own Little Way

A Collection of Poems

Paul Collison

Austin Macauley Publishers
London * Cambridge * New York * Sharjah

Copyright © **Paul Collison** (2021)

The right of **Paul Collison** to be identified as author of this work has been asserted by the author in accordance with section 77 and 78 of the Copyright, Designs and Patents Act 1988.

All rights reserved. No part of this publication may be reproduced, stored in a retrieval system, or transmitted in any form or by any means, electronic, mechanical, photocopying, recording, or otherwise, without the prior permission of the publishers.

Any person who commits any unauthorised act in relation to this publication may be liable to criminal prosecution and civil claims for damages.

A CIP catalogue record for this title is available from the British Library.

ISBN 9781528994798 (Paperback)
ISBN 9781528995238 (ePub e-book)

www.austinmacauley.com

First Published (2021)
Austin Macauley Publishers Ltd
25 Canada Square
Canary Wharf
London
E14 5LQ

To my wife Julie and my late mother Carol.

A Change of Season

Autumn arrives as summer fades,
Leaves fall like promises made.
The seasons move on,
And so we do too.
All things come to pass,
Between me and you.
There's a difference now,
In the sky up above.
I wonder why,
There's an end to our love.
Time doesn't stand still,
And neither should we.
The seasons must change,
That's what we must see.

A Duck at Dawn

He treads a path across Cardiff,
Looking for a meal.
He dodges drunken strangers,
Out looking for a deal.
He raids around the waste bins,
Looking for some snack,
Eyes alive to danger,
In case of an attack.
He finds a bag of crisps,
A rare and sweet delight.
He munches for an hour,
Then he's home 'til night.

A Ghost in the Corridors

He arises from his bed,
In the middle of the night.
Those paid to observe the ritual,
Glance, disinterestedly, from their chairs.
He is no threat and of little interest.
Every night he wanders the corridors.
No light behind his eyes,
His lifeless body passes with no sound.
As he reappears no one looks,
Does he even exist at all?
Against the clinical backdrop,
And into clean white sheets,
His withered body resumes its
living death.

A Haunting

When I shut out the light,
I can still see her face.
Though years have passed,
I can find no peace.
She appears from nowhere,
And fades as I faint.
No remorse on her lips,
As she taunts me once more.
I know not why I am chosen;
To suffer this fate.
There is no meaning,
And no reason.
Nonetheless, I bear the burden,
Of callous haunting and death will be
my freedom.

A Lock of Hair

You cut the first lock of hair from my head,
And put in an envelope.
You always believed in me,
When I felt no hope.
That lock was returned to me,
When you slept for eternity.
It's in a box with those things you loved,
And that meant so much to you.
I keep all your precious memories;
They remind me of the love we shared.
My love for you is endless,
And forever growing.
Though we share different worlds,
My heart beats forever to your drum.
We are not lost to each other,
And time has no meaning.
We are apart only by awful fate,
I will come to you if you can only wait;
Just mere moments and I am with you
forever more.

A Poem for Autumn

The leaves that fall upon my shoulders,
Are a blanket against the gentle chill.
The trees send this gift,
So I know I'm not alone.
As I walk the quiet streets,
The world is changing all around me.
I must change too,
As the wonder of the seasons brings hope.

A River's Journey

The river flows by twisting roads,
Meandering through villages and towns.
Its silvery sheen and the creatures unseen,
Progress down the hill with no sound.
Past cats catching fish,
And dogs chasing sticks,
It runs through its usual course.
The river lives on after all else has gone,
Flowing great with such enviable force.

A Tale from the Asylum

I opened the pack up,
With a sensational break.
Your cue in one hand,
You stepped up to the plate.
You went straight for the black,
With a brutal attack.

You declared your win,
Bewildered I smiled.
Your happiness broad,
As if you're a child.
We shook hands and connected,
And no longer rejected.
I accepted defeat,
And hoped for a life.

Do You Hear It?

Can you hear that sound?
The music that plays,
I hear it all around.
The melodies once heard,
Repeat their patterns.
They help me when I get lost,
In a wave of sadness.
I lock myself into the joy,
Of endless love that music brings.
There is only light ahead now,
And delightful sound surrounds me.

Existence on the Extremes

You can't see me,
But I can see you.
I have reached out,
With arms parted,
To seek a friend.
There is not one to be found.
No reply as my voice grows weak.
I am old and weary,
And my slow death is a bitter affair.
Once, I had life and flourished.
But I was born to die in silence,
And my name 'Cymru',
To be remembered nevermore.

For Vincent

Your music lives forever,
And flows through all our lives.
Enchanting all that find it,
The heartfelt and the wise.
Mesmerising notes of wonder,
Beguiling throughout time.
Your beauty never fades,
As your organ sweetly chimes.

From Darkness

'The trouble with taking a photograph is
that which should never be seen is indeed
seen, and never can be unseen.'
I looked directly at you and never once did
I see your piercing bright eyes.
You saw me, saw through me and into me
with that brilliance and cunning of mind.
I know you now and also I know you were
with me every step of the way;
Before you crossed my path and let it be
known you were satisfied I was
hurried away.
I won't come back, too much has been said
with your stare.
I must be as if nothing to you, yet you
must have known I would capture
your image.
I will never enter your lair and no more
shall I look upon your form.

That you exist pains me and life is as if
a dream.
You have spared me and somehow
I endure.
Peace must always be with you, I am sure
of that.
Maybe you have always been with us
and will always inhabit those areas we
shouldn't visit.
In daylight you have appeared and
night-time has fallen for me.

Ghosts of Stalingrad

There's no more fighting,
No more flames.
On the banks of the Volga,
They sit and wait for the Sun to set.
The ghosts of Stalingrad rise to dance
and sing;
No enemies remain.
Hands are held,
Locked in love.
All who have fallen rise again when
night descends.
They finish the dance and bodies, freed
from pain,

Step to the water's edge.
Together, they cross the Volga,
Under the moonlit sky.
As they disappear from view,
They ascend from the far bank of the river;
They look down upon the factories, houses
and colourful lights of their beloved city.
Brothers and sisters, lost in battle, are
friends in death.

Gwenllian

She never knew her name and signed it
'Wentliane'. This is for our beloved
last princess...

Princess Gwenllian born out of love,
Watch over your children from your home
in the stars.
Beloved, eternal Princess of Wales,
No high walls can surround you now.
Hidden from the world in life, you are
hidden no more and are free.
We love and treasure you for eternity and
you are no longer lost.
We have found you and you have found us,
and we carry you in our hearts forever.

Journeys

A journey on a bus,
Is no easy thing.
Nothing is pleasant,
And no heart can sing.
Terrible people,
Crawl in from the cold.
Their bigoted hatred,
For me to behold.
There is no hiding,
From the repulsive assault.
Nobody helps me,
I guess it's my fault.

Life in the Mop

As I ready myself to clean the floor,
Just like all of those times before.
I see you wriggle around,
Then you fall to the ground.
A grey little chap,
Once taking a nap,
Now running for life,
Through convenient gaps.
More of you fall from the mop,
I skip and I hop,
To save the day,
In my own little way.
With a shake you are freed,
And you run taking heed,
Of the perilous landscape,
And creeping fatigue.
I wait for a while,
And look with a smile,
As you hurry away,
To inevitable freedom,
And a new place to stay.

Poles

They stand so strong and tall,
They'll never bow or fall.
They watch over the hills,
Where trees and rivers fill.

They're there forever more,
However rich or poor.
A constant to our eyes,
A beauty none despise.

They reach so far, so high,
The trees but wonder why.
Their metal friends exist,
Forever they resist.

Resist

I will resist in the morning,
And through the day, 'til night.
I can always be depended on,
To carry on the fight.
There's no mountain I can't climb,
I always will resist.
No cold words ever tempt me,
From those that still persist,
In spreading furious hate,
And expecting us to fall.
My steps will never falter,
'til I break down every wall.

Small Worlds

So many snails,
Come out to play,
In their dark 'pot world',
Hidden away.
Out of sight and out of fright,
Break of day,
Or dead of night.
Their world is dark,
Yet full of light.

The Forest

The forest reaches wide and far,
Atop the mountainside.
The woods that live inside my heart,
My love I cannot hide.
They shroud themselves in mystery,
And call out to your soul.
Through tales of dreadful history,
They live on, one and all.

It's heaven when you're strolling,
Through endless trees of joy.
The fields they keep on rolling,
As man becomes a boy.

The Future and the Past

If you look at the past,
You can see the future.
It's all there behind us,
Awaiting before us.
If you look at the sea,
As it washes ashore.
You're seeing what millions,
Have witnessed before.
If you walk up a mountain,
You're passing through time.
Treading the countless footsteps,
Just like yours and mine.
Yet, we learn so little,
Remember much less.
We are left here to flounder,
Under duress.

The Sea's Lament

At low tide the sea seems so far away,
As if she will never arrive.
At high tide, she seems so in distress,

As her waves crash and die.
She will come again another day,
Always the same routine.
Unbroken by this turbulence,
She hides her hurt unseen.

The Sun's Vision

The Sun shines so high above me,
Gazing at the Earth through our beautiful blue sky.
He observes the stars and the limitless space,
Wonders who, what, how or why?
He sees all for eternity and knows all worlds;
He encounters great comets, meteors and all.

He smiles as they pass him, as he'll never fall.
He's always awake to someone, somewhere,
He shines for eternity and smiles at the scene.